Seattle World School
Seattle, Washington

WORLD WAR II U.S. HOMEFRONT

WITHDRAWN

A HISTORY PERSPECTIVES BOOK

Martin Gitlin

Published in the United States of America
by Cherry Lake Publishing
Ann Arbor, Michigan
www.cherrylakepublishing.com

Consultants: Allan M. Winkler, University Distinguished Professor of History, Miami University,
Oxford, Ohio; Marla Conn, ReadAbility, Inc.
Editorial direction: Red Line Editorial
Book design: Sleeping Bear Press

Photo Credits: U.S. Army Air Corps/Library of Congress, cover (left), 1 (left); Ann Rosener/
Library of Congress, cover (middle), 1 (middle), 12; Russell Lee/Library of Congress, cover
(right), 1 (right), 22; David Bransby/Library of Congress, 4; Andreas Feininger/Library of
Congress, 6; Library of Congress, 9; Bettmann/Corbis, 11, 14; U.S. Army Signal Corps/Associated
Press, 15; Jack Delano/Library of Congress, 18; Arthur Siegel/Library of Congress, 21; Dorothea
Lange/Library of Congress, 24, 26; Horace Bristol/Corbis, 28; Service/epa/Corbis, 30

Library of Congress Cataloging-in-Publication Data
Gitlin, Martin.
 World War II U.S. homefront / Martin Gitlin.
    pages cm. -- (Perspectives library)
 Includes index.
 ISBN 978-1-63137-621-4 (hardcover) -- ISBN 978-1-63137-666-5 (pbk.) -- ISBN 978-1-63137-
711-2 (pdf ebook) -- ISBN 978-1-63137-756-3 (hosted ebook)
1. World War, 1939–1945--United States--Juvenile literature. 2. World War, 1939–1945--Social
aspects--United States--Juvenile literature. 3. United States--Social conditions--1933–1945--
Juvenile literature. I. Title.
D769.1.G57 2014
940.53'73--dc23

                         2014004588

Cherry Lake Publishing would like to acknowledge the work of
The Partnership for 21st Century Skills. Please visit *www.p21.org*
for more information.

Printed in the United States of America
Corporate Graphics Inc.
July 2014

TABLE OF CONTENTS

In this book, you will read about the lives of three U.S. civilians during World War II. Many people faced personal struggles and hardships during this period in the early 1940s. As you'll see, the same event can look different depending on one's point of view.

Eleanor Lewis

Bomber Plant Worker

I am feeling many emotions today. It is September 11, 1942. I kissed my husband, Joe, goodbye exactly eight months ago today. He went off to man the USS *Cushing*, a navy destroyer near the island of Guadalcanal in the Pacific. Every day I pray that Japanese forces have not killed him. That is my biggest fear. Only his letters give me hope for his safety.

ROSIE THE RIVETER

A popular 1942 song first used the term "Rosie the Riveter." The song portrays a female factory worker doing what she can to help the U.S. war effort. Rosie the Riveter began to represent all working women during World War II. A cover for the *Saturday Evening Post*, painted by Norman Rockwell, also made the image of the female factory worker famous during the war.

But that is not the only reason I am frightened. I also fear for my country's safety. Japan showed how easily it could attack U.S. territory when it bombed Pearl Harbor last December. The Germans have overrun all of Europe and taken over much of the Soviet Union. It is plain to see that Adolf Hitler and

▲ *A team of men and women build a B-17 heavy bomber airplane in 1942.*

the **Axis Powers** will stop at nothing to rule the world. I am scared that the war will eventually spill onto the U.S. mainland.

I try to remember what President Franklin D. Roosevelt said in his speech in January 1933 after winning the election. He calmed Americans about the Great Depression by claiming that there was nothing to fear but fear itself. I wish I could convince myself of that when it comes to this war. But the Japanese dropped bombs in Oregon forests just the other day. I know they did not do much damage, but I still feel threatened, even here in Detroit, Michigan.

So how do I show my strong sense of U.S. pride? I am doing my part in the war effort. I work at the Willow Run Bomber Plant making parts for B-29 and B-24 **bomber planes**. We just completed manufacturing our first B-24 bomber. This work gives me a feeling of purpose. Folks wonder if women will quit their jobs and return to being housewives when the war is over. I am not sure I want to.

I certainly wouldn't want to stay at Willow Run, though. Why should women be paid less than half of what the men make doing the same work? I was gabbing with a man last week and he revealed his salary. It is more than twice what I earn. He was hired the same day as me and also had no experience, yet his job title is engineer and I am a worker's aide.

SECOND SOURCE

▶ Find another source on the pay of women in factories during World War II. Compare the information there to the information in this source.

I did not complain at first. I was afraid to rock the boat. But I finally confronted my boss. He told me sternly that working for less money was better than not working at all. It was obvious that he was threatening to fire me.

My low pay at Willow Run makes me mad, but it is my job as a mother that has me

▲ *B-24 bombers were heavily used during World War II to drop bombs and deliver cargo to troops.*

overwhelmed. My daughter, Maureen, is six years old. She is too young to be left alone, but there are times I must abandon her, even through the night. I have left her crying in her bed because I have been forced to work a night shift when I cannot find a babysitter. I sob all the way to work. I have no choice. We need the money for food, rent, and clothing.

My heart breaks for Maureen, but I feel as though I am being torn in five different directions. When I am not working, I am often shopping for groceries. Even that is difficult. The government **rations** things like sugar, butter, meat, and even gasoline and tires for my car. Sometimes I cannot find certain things at the nearby store because there are shortages.

THINK ABOUT IT

▶ Read this chapter carefully. What surprises you about this perspective? Discuss this with a friend or classmate.

▲ *Americans used ration stamps to buy food that was in short supply during the war.*

▲ *Many families and groups grew vegetables and fruit in their victory gardens.*

So I have to drive elsewhere to buy them. I have no time for myself.

The one activity Maureen and I have been working on together is the victory garden in our tiny backyard. We had a bumper crop this summer. We raised carrots, tomatoes, and green beans. Maureen thinks they taste better than the vegetables we used to buy at the store. I feel proud that our victory garden allows U.S. farmers to send more food to feed our soldiers.

I wish there was some other way to help the war effort. My cousin Gloria in New York helps run the Stage Door Canteen. It is a nightspot where soldiers can have a little fun before going off to war. It just opened in early March. Maybe I can ask Gloria if I can move in with her and help her run the nightspot. I must help the war effort. But I also have to earn enough money to take care of Maureen and myself. I don't know what to do.

Willie Johnson

Grocery Clerk

It was exactly 1:23 p.m. on October 23, 1943, when we got the news. I know because I glanced at the clock. I was putting cans of peas on the shelves when my little brother Leroy ran into the grocery store where I work. He held up a letter and was very excited.

"It's from Sam! It's from Sam!" he yelled to me. He was talking about my best friend,

Sam Rackley. Leroy loves and respects Sam as much as I do. Sam is training to be a bomber **escort** pilot at Selfridge Field in Detroit, Michigan, as part of the Tuskegee Institute Airman program. I know all about it. We both participated in the Civilian Pilot Training Program at the Tuskegee Institute here in Alabama in 1940.

▲ *Cadets at the Tuskegee Institute line up for inspection by Major James A. Ellison in 1942.*

I feel jealous of Sam. We are both 23 years old, but he is doing something thrilling and important with his life. He told me all about it in his letter. He has been working with the 332nd Fighter Group.

His unit moved from Tuskegee to Detroit in March. He will soon be escorting bombers overseas. He will be helping his country defeat the Axis Powers in this terrible war. What am I doing? I'm putting

THE TUSKEGEE AIRMEN IN ACTION

The 332nd Fighter Group began World War II combat operations in Italy in June 1943. They flew 1,578 missions over the next year. They never lost a bomber to enemy aircraft. Commander Benjamin Davis later became a three-star general in the Army Air Corps.

cans of peas and corn on a grocery shelf in Montgomery, Alabama.

Not that Sam has had it easy. He wrote that the training has been tough. He added that his commanding officers, Colonels Robert Selway and William Boyd, **discriminated** against black people like Sam and me. They refused to allow black airmen to mix socially with whites. But I am proud to report that Sam and his fellow black officers stood up to the colonels. Now a black colonel, Benjamin Davis, commands Sam's bomber group.

What has me excited is that Sam wants me to join him at Selfridge Field for bomber training. He believes I will be accepted because I graduated with him from the Civilian Pilot Training Program.

When I returned home from work today, I talked to my father about it. He is dead set against it. He wonders why I would want to fight for a country that discriminates against people like us.

I understand his reasoning. We have no true freedom here in Alabama. The Civil War has been over for nearly 80 years and black people are still blocked from voting. We cannot attend the same schools as whites. Our schools are just little shacks while the white children go to classes in big, clean, beautiful buildings.

▲ *African Americans had to wait in a separate "Colored" waiting room at a bus station in North Carolina.*

We are denied access to restaurants, pools, bus stations, and even public bathrooms.

My father reminded me today about his friend Tom. Two years ago, Tom demanded service at an all-white restaurant. He caused quite a scene. The next day my father found Tom hanging dead from a tree. He had been **lynched**. The police in Montgomery did nothing about it.

I know that racial problems extend beyond the South. Sam described a race riot that occurred right there in Detroit in June. It started with small fights between white and black teenagers and ended in terrible violence on both sides.

The riots lasted a couple days and all but shut down

SECOND SOURCE

▶ Find another source on the treatment of African Americans in the South during the 1940s. Compare the information there to the information in this source.

the city. Sam said that white policemen were shooting at black people in the street. By the time it was over, 25 blacks and nine whites were dead. He told me that 17 of those blacks were killed by white police officers. This is one of the most awful incidents I have ever heard about. It makes me realize that racism against blacks is not limited to the South.

I can understand why my father does not want me to fight for the United States. But if we blacks as a group prove our love for our country and our ability in combat, we can help end racial discrimination when we return home. Even in Alabama, where discrimination is at its worst, I believe we will no longer be denied our rights if we fight for the United States. Maybe we can even change our world.

THINK ABOUT IT

▶ Determine the main point of the chapter. Pick out one piece of evidence that supports it.

My father and I talked about that. I think
I softened him up a bit. He is still against me becoming
a fighter pilot and going off to war. Perhaps it is as
much because he is afraid I'll be killed as any moral
reasons. My father told me that he will accept whatever
decision I make.

▲ *A 1942 race riot broke out in Detroit, Michigan, when whites did not want*
African Americans to move into the Sojourner Truth housing project, named
for the famous nineteenth century antislavery activist.

Miyoshi Takahara

Japanese American

No American felt more **patriotism** and anger on December 7, 1941, than I did. I was born and raised in this country, though my parents came from Japan. I have been living in San Diego, California, for nearly 20 years. And when the Japanese bombed Pearl Harbor that morning, a love for my country swelled up inside of me. I was as mad at the Japanese leaders who ordered the attack as any of my American neighbors.

I stood up and cheered when I heard President Roosevelt declare war with Japan on the radio. Sure, I was worried about my relatives living in Tokyo. But I knew going to war was the right thing to do. I had no fear that my fellow Americans would turn against me because of my Japanese background. I assumed they thought of my family as Americans.

I assumed wrong. A week after the attack a group of boys beat up my six-year-old son, Joseph, after school. They called him a "dirty Jap" and gave him a black eye. Many local citizens boycotted Takahara Hardware, a store run by my husband, Hiroko, and me. We lost quite a bit of our business. And suddenly our white friends stopped coming to our house for visits. When we see them on the street now, they act as if they are frightened of us. They treat us like we are spies.

▲ *A store owned by Japanese Americans posted a patriotic sign in their window the day after the Pearl Harbor bombing.*

We have taken steps to show that we are patriotic Americans. We bragged to everyone that we bought war bonds. We began to fly the U.S. flag outside our home and placed one on the window of our store.

We even changed the name of our business to Star Spangled Hardware. But some customers leave as soon as they see that we are Japanese.

At first, I just thought these anti-Japanese feelings would blow over. But now I am more worried than ever, not just for my family. I am deeply concerned for every Japanese American on the West Coast.

On January 20, I read an **editorial** in the *San Diego Union* claiming Japanese Americans could not be real Americans. I cried because I knew I was as American as any white person. I felt a sense of dread when I read letters to the editor. They requested that all people of Japanese descent be removed from the West Coast of the United States.

They were just ignorant people. But I got scared when city leaders began saying the

SECOND SOURCE

▶ Find a second source about how Japanese Americans were treated during World War II. Compare that source with the information here.

▲ *Signs posted told people of Japanese descent to report to government centers so that they could be eventually sent to camps away from the coast.*

same thing. A day after that editorial appeared in the paper, the city council sent a **resolution** to the Federal Bureau of Investigation. It stated that Japanese people in the area were dangers to the community. They claimed they had proof that some Japanese people were anti-American.

I have several friends in the United States who once lived in Japan. One of them sent their children to a Japanese language school that the federal government shut down last month. Yet not one has expressed anything but love for this country. Japanese leaders have encouraged us to comply with the government to prove that we are patriotic Americans.

The federal government has already begun detaining Japanese people they consider dangerous. But that is not enough to satisfy some leaders. A local board passed a resolution stating that all Japanese should be at least 100 miles away from the San Diego city center. They worry that Japanese Americans might be somehow helping Japan plan attacks against the West Coast. The League of California Cities urged all its members to pass similar resolutions.

ANALYZE THIS

▶ Analyze two of the accounts of people living in the United States during World War II in this book. How are they different? How are they the same?

▲ *Thousands of people of Japanese descent were sent to live in remote **internment** camps during the war.*

The public's fear of Japanese Americans has become normal in this country. President Roosevelt received a letter from a group of congressmen urging an order that every Japanese citizen be removed from areas along the West Coast.

I can only hope and pray that our leaders don't act upon such a horrible request. I am afraid we are going to lose our home and business. I am afraid for my child. I am afraid of the future. Before the attack on Pearl Harbor, we were living the American dream. Now we are living an American nightmare. And there is nothing we can do about it.

JAPANESE AMERICAN INTERNMENT

About 117,000 Japanese Americans living on the West Coast were detained during World War II. Two-thirds of them were born in the United States. They were ordered to government centers near their homes. Then they were sent to internment camps. They were really prison camps, such as Topaz and Manzanar, far from the West Coast. Many Japanese Americans had to live in the camps until the end of the war.

LOOK, LOOK AGAIN

This photo shows the bombing of Pearl Harbor on December 7, 1941. Use this photograph to answer the following questions:

1. What would a female bomber plant worker say about this picture? How would she describe this scene to her coworkers?

2. How would an African American man describe the bombing? What would he discuss with his friends and family about the picture?

3. What would a Japanese American person think about this image? How might that person feel after seeing it?

GLOSSARY

Axis Powers (AK-siss POU-urz) a group of countries united during World War II that included Germany, Japan, and Italy

bomber plane (BAH-mer PLAYN) a plane that attempts to drop a bomb directly on or near enough to damage a target

discriminate (diss-KRIM-uh-nate) to treat a person or group of people unfairly

editorial (ed-uh-TOR-ee-uhl) an article or statement that reflects a person's opinion

escort (ESS-kort) a plane that accompanies and protects other planes

internment (in-TURN-muhnt) relating to forced confinement, often during war

lynch (LINCH) to kill someone illegally, especially by hanging

patriotism (PAY-tree-uh-tizm) love and support for one's country

ration (RASH-uhn) to control the amount of something, such as food, in order to limit how much people are allowed to have of that item

resolution (rez-uh-LOO-shun) a firm decision to do or not do something

LEARN MORE

Further Reading

George, Linda, and Charles George. *The Tuskegee Airmen.* New York: Children's Press, 2001.

Roppelt, Donna. *Women Go to Work, 1941–1945.* Philadelphia: Mason Crest Publishers, 2013.

Sandler, Martin W. *Imprisoned: The Betrayal of Japanese Americans during World War II.* New York: Walker Books for Young Readers, 2013.

Web Sites

National Park Service. Rosie the Riveter: Women Working During World War II
http://www.nps.gov/pwro/collection/website/home.htm
This Web site has information about the contributions of U.S. women working during World War II.

National World War II Museum: The Tuskegee Airmen
http://www.nationalww2museum.org/learn/education/for-students/ww2-history/at-a-glance/tuskegee-airmen.html
Learn about the Tuskegee airmen and how they were involved during World War II on this Web site.

INDEX

ABOUT THE AUTHOR

Martin Gitlin is an educational book writer. He has authored approximately 80 books for children, many about U.S. history, including an interactive book about the homefront during World War II. Gitlin lives with his wife and three children in Cleveland, Ohio.